SUMMARY

of

THE GREAT GATSBY

A FastReads Summary with Key Takeaways & Analysis

NOTE: The purpose of this FastReads summary is to help you decide if it's worth the time, money and effort reading the original book (if you haven't already). FastReads has pulled out the essence with commentary and critique—but only to help you ascertain the value of the book for yourself. This summary is meant to be a supplement to, and not a replacement for the original book

Follow this link to purchase a copy of the original book on Amazon.

TABLE OF CONTENTS

EXECUTIVE SUMMARY

In *The Great Gatsby,* Fitzgerald explores the resistance, decadence, and exuberance of people during what's popularly known as the Jazz Age. The book failed to garner a lot of attention initially when it was published in 1925, but now after almost a century, it has not only been remade into a major feature film, but it's also considered the holy grail in American literary fiction.

What makes the book so special is that it encapsulates love, victory, and tragedy beautifully. As the economy grew in the 1920s, people began to lead more opulent lives, and the story serves as a snapshot of the American Society that was changing rapidly. It was an era where wealth flowed freely, but it was also a period that was the most chaotic in American history. Nick Carraway—Jay Gatsby's neighbor—narrates the story, and Fitzgerald describes how Gatsby's unabating desire to get his lost love back in his life pushes him towards an unfortunate ending.

INTRODUCTION

During the 1920s, American Society experienced a dramatic change regarding economy. In fact, people began to shed their rigid inhibitions of the past and embraced their golden future with open arms. With money flowing in the country, people began to spend more on consumer goods like never before. Suddenly, opportunities were abundant everywhere, and people rejoiced in their newfound financial freedom.

Fitzgerald describes how people led lives filled with excess, and hardworking people like Gatsby seized all the opportunities to amass wealth beyond their dreams. The story takes place in West Egg where Gatsby has a house near his long-lost love—Daisy Buchanan. She's married to Tom Buchanan whose arrogant attitude and adultery is the talk of the town. Nick moves to East Egg to seek his fortune and his views on the people surrounding him give the reader an inkling of the society that was rampant with greed and betrayal.

Key Takeaways

• *The Great Gatsby* describes how Jay Gatsby moved heaven and earth to get the woman he loved back into his life.

• Post WWI, American Society witnessed great prosperity in the Jazz Age, but it was also the most corrupt period where greed was extremely dominant.

CHAPTER 1

As a child, Nick Carraway learned from his father to never criticize others. He also learned to reserve his judgments since most people don't have all the advantages they deserve. Nick recollects the events that unfolded almost a year ago when Jay Gatsby was his neighbor. In 1922, Nick traveled from the Midwest to a small town named West Egg that was located on Long Island, New York.

Nick had a comfortable childhood thanks to his wealthy family, and after he had returned from WWI, he wanted to pursue a career as a bond trader on Wall Street. He was confident because of his wealth, and his degree from the Yale University made him consider himself superior to most people. West Egg boasted of several rich inhabitants, and Nick's cozy house was nestled amidst numerous large mansions. However, East Egg was considered superior since it housed people with "old money."

Nick's cousin, Daisy Buchanan, and her husband, Tom Buchanan, live in a fantabulous mansion in East Egg, and Nick meets them. He is then invited to dinner where he learns that Tom—who was also his acquaintance in college—hasn't changed much at all. Tom is still the muscular, aggressive, loudmouthed man he was when he was young, but he appears even more despicable as a racist now. Nick, however, is jubilant to see Daisy, and she receives him warmly too.

As the evening progresses, Nick is introduced to Jordan Baker—a woman flaunting a lithe, sleek body as a professional golfer—and he is instantly attracted to her. Nick tries to get comfortable with them, but the incessant ringing of the telephone interrupts them several times. Tom leaves the table to take the phone call as Daisy stares at them ashen faced. She then decides to confront Tom and leaves the room. Jordan tells Nick about Tom's affairs with his mistress even as she unabashedly tries to listen to the couple quarreling.

It is obvious that Nick is a little uncomfortable with everything happening around him, but he says nothing. He is merely an observer. Although the dinner is awkward, he politely gets on with it without any complaints. After Nick leaves to go back to his house, he is mesmerized by a dark figure in Gatsby's house. Nick remains silent as the man stretches his arms out to a green light shining at the dock's end. The green light is shining from the dock at Tom and Daisy's house, but before Nick can do anything, Gatsby vanishes.

Key Takeaways

• Nick Carraway meets Tom Buchanan and Daisy in their palatial home in East Egg.

• Nick isn't very comfortable with the rich and snobbish people around him.

CHAPTER 2

As Nick and Tom travel to New York on a train one evening, they come across a desolate valley dumped with ashes. Nick watches as the men shovel the ashes retrieved from the coal furnaces. It seems that the valley is lifeless and torn, but the men continue to work without complaining. An old billboard featuring the eyes of an optometrist named T.J Eckleburg draws Nick's attention, and it seems as though the doctor's watchful eyes are registering everything that occurs in the valley.

The train chugs along and makes several stops in its journey from West Egg to New York, and Tom suddenly decides to meet his mistress. He further forces Nick to accompany him, and they get off the train. Nick runs along to catch up with Tom as he walks into Wilson's garage. George Wilson—a and lifeless yet handsome man who almost looks gray because of the ashes—is unaware of his wife Myrtle's affair with Tom and talks to him about business.

Myrtle arrives down the stairs even as Tom and Wilson chat away. She's a sensuous, stocky, well-dressed woman who is the opposite of her husband. Although she isn't really beautiful, she carries herself well, and Tom slyly glances at her. Wilson seems lost, but she is alive and ready to live life as much as she can. She instructs Wilson to grab some chairs, and he obliges.

Myrtle immediately stalks towards Tom and touches him. Tom is drawn to her even as Nick watches them. Tom introduces her to Nick, and Wilson—unaware of everything happening right under his nose—keeps talking. Tom hands Myrtle some money and orders her to take a train to New York. Tom invites Nick too, and although he refuses, he insists until Nick accepts.

Tom, Nick, and Myrtle head to Tom's apartment that's reserved especially for his affairs. Myrtle invites her sister Catherine and other friends and they all party even as Nick seems a little miffed. He tries to leave, but Tom refuses to let him go. As the party continues further, Catherine informs Nick that Gatsby is Kaiser Wilhelm's cousin who ruled Germany during WWI.

Tom, Myrtle and the others behave outrageously, spilling drinks on everyone, and even as Nick feels repelled, he is also fascinated by everyone around him. At one point, he feels that he's having the best time ever, but he also feels sick to watch them all. On the other hand, Myrtle mentions Daisy continuously, and Tom retaliates by punching and breaking her nose. Nick finally leaves and hops on a train to get back home.

Key Takeaways

• Nick finds that Tom not only has illicit affairs with other women but he doesn't bother to hide them either.

• Tom takes Nick to an apartment he's reserved for his affairs and a party begins, and although Nick is fascinated by everyone, he also feels sick and repulsive towards them.

CHAPTER 3

By now, Nick is familiar with Gatsby's fetish to host extravagant parties. Most men and women ended up at the parties even when they weren't invited. Gatsby is famous for not inviting anyone, so Nick is understandably shocked when he receives a hand-written invitation from none other than Gatsby.

Nick agrees and joins the party that's already brimming with guests. People enjoy themselves and even strangers merrily access the champagne and drinks that flow endlessly throughout the party. While some jump into the pool, others dance the night away. The dazzling lights, flowers, and chandeliers exhibit Gatsby's richness, and Nick observes them all.

He tries to find Gatsby, but interestingly, nobody seems to know where he is, making it obvious that they have never met him. It's interesting that people use Gatsby's pool and everything else in his house even though they've never seen him! Nick is so embarrassed that he proceeds to get drunk. Suddenly, Jordan Baker approaches him and they both mill around aimlessly, listening to several rumors floating around about Gatsby suggesting that he's a German spy and once killed a man.

Nick treats himself to champagne and meets a stranger. They begin to talk, and Nick tells him that Gatsby invited him. The stranger suddenly introduces himself, and Nick is embarrassed to know that the stranger is none other than Gatsby. He observes that Gatsby is a young man and his speech is so formal that it almost seems absurd. A butler interrupts their conversation, and Gatsby leaves them, promising to talk to Nick later. Nick demands more information from Jordan about Gatsby, but she knows nothing about him apart from the fact that he went to Oxford.

The orchestra leader plays a new song and the crowd cheers while Nick notices Gatsby observing people in the party. Nick wonders if he could have killed a man, but decides that there's nothing sinister about him. Gatsby appears elegant with his tanned skin and short hair. It's evident that he takes care of himself and the fact that he's not drinking makes him a class apart from his guests.

Gatsby's butler comes to Jordan and tells her that Gatsby wants to discuss something private with her. She's surprised and leaves Nick alone to join Gatsby. Nick observes that the hilarity of the party ceases to end as most people begin to fight with each other. Inebriated and hopeless, many women are forced by their husbands to leave the party. Nick is about to leave when Jordan joins him and tells him that she heard something amazing from Gatsby. She then leaves after inviting Nick to meet her. Gatsby comes to Nick and Nick politely apologizes again for not recognizing him earlier. Gatsby reassures him and reminds him to meet him the next morning.

Key Takeaways

• Gatsby is famous for his bold parties but he rarely invites anyone, so Nick is shocked to find a hand-written note from Gatsby inviting him to his next soiree.

• Nick finally meets Gatsby and finds him very charismatic.

CHAPTER 4

Nick recounts all the famous people he meets at Gatsby's parties. The Leeches, Ismays, Chester Becker, Chrysties, etc.—just about everybody attends his parties even when they know zilch about him. One morning, Gatsby suddenly arrives at Nick's house to have lunch with him. As Gatsby drives the car, he tries to clear any misunderstandings or assumptions Nick may have developed, which gives a subtle hint that he's aware of the rumors about him.

Nick listens to everything Gatsby has to say but slowly begins to grow suspicious, especially when Gatsby mentions that he attended Oxford. Gatsby seems uncomfortable when he talks about Oxford, thereby giving Nick a distinct impression that he's lying. Nick recounts how Jordan felt the same way and understands why she may have felt so. Gatsby also boasts that he served in the military as a major, and even when he tried desperately to die, he somehow led an enchanted life. At that point, Gatsby drives really fast, and Nick becomes even more uncomfortable. An officer pulls them over; however, much to Nick's astonishment, they are let go without any questions simply because Gatsby produces a card he's received from the commissioner of police when he'd bestowed a favor upon him.

Later, Gatsby takes Nick to meet Meyer Wolfshiem—a professional gambler rumored to have connections with organized crime. Nick finds him peculiar and expressive, and as they continue to converse with each other, Wolfshiem talks about Nick's business interests. Nick looks confused, but Gatsby clears the air and says that Wolfshiem has the wrong man. Later, as they prepare to leave, Nick notices Tom in the crowd and talks him. Suddenly, Gatsby seems all embarrassed and strained—a quality Nick has never seen in him. Nick keeps talking to Tom, but as he turns to Gatsby, he's surprised that he's no longer there.

One day, Nick meets Jordan, and she recounts how an unknown military officer—Jay Gatsby—had pursued Daisy. She also recollects that he looked at her in a way every young woman yearned to be looked at. Daisy seemed to love him too, but she shifted her attention to Tom Buchanan after her parents disapproved of her affair. She did think about reconsidering her decision, but after a short tantrum, she just let it go and reluctantly married Tom.

Jordan tells Nick about Daisy and Tom's daughter, and she continues to relay the conversation she had with Gatsby the other night. Incredibly, Gatsby was so much in love with Daisy that he had shifted to West Egg only because he wanted to be close to her. Everything he did had a purpose, and it revolved around Daisy and her interests. Looking into Nick's eyes, Jordan asks if he can invite Daisy over to his house so that Gatsby can see her. She also requests Nick not to share the information with Daisy as Gatsby wants it all to be a pleasant surprise.

Key Takeaways

• Nick, suspicious of Gatsby's background, finds it hard to believe when Gatsby tells him that he was educated at Oxford.

• Nick learns that Daisy and Gatsby separated years ago when her parents disliked Gatsby.

CHAPTER 5

Later that night, Gatsby walks up to Nick as soon as he returns home. Nick is perplexed to see Gatsby's house blazing with all the lights on. Gatsby, eager to talk to him, invites him to Coney Island, but Nick declines. Nick then mentions that he will call Daisy the next morning, and Gatsby tries his best to control his emotions. He hesitates a moment and tries tactlessly to offer Nick some money, but Nick cuts him short and declines the offer again.

The next day, Nick invites Daisy to his place but warns her to come alone. Later, on the appointed day, Daisy arrives at Nick's home only to see various types of flowers adorning his home. Nick looks for Gatsby and quickly realizes that he has disappeared, but later, he finds Gatsby at his front door, appearing tragic and unsettled.

Gatsby walks into Nick's home and finally meets the woman of his dreams. The reunion seems stilted at first and the trio feel awkward, but as the day progresses, they become comfortable with each other. Nick, aware of their needs, excuses himself and leaves the room but Gatsby follows him in his nervousness. Nick sends him back after reminding him that it's rude to leave Daisy alone and slinks out the back door to give them some privacy.

As Nick goes back to his house, he notices that Gatsby is a completely changed man. All his nervousness seems to have vanished, and his eyes shine in delight as he listens to his love murmuring intimately. It seems as if they were never apart from each other. Nick notices that they are so lost in each other that they radiate a sort of warmth that is immediately evident to an observer. Later, they shift to Gatsby's house upon his request, and Daisy is floored by the sheer elegance of the house.

Gatsby, proud of his home, takes them from one room to another while Daisy expresses her delight over everything she sees. After going through his initial embarrassment and indescribable joy, he now enters a third phase: wonder at her presence. Gatsby cannot believe that Daisy has finally arrived at his home and he does everything to impress her. Daisy also appears to be extremely happy to have met Gatsby as the thrill in her voice is obvious. She also notices Gatsby's beautiful shirts and is completely in awe of him. As the day wears on, Gatsby manages to show off everything he has much to Daisy's delight. They seem to be so engrossed in each other that they almost ignore Nick. Nick, understanding their need for privacy, leaves the lovebirds and returns to his home.

Key Takeaways

• Nick declines Gatsby's financial help but invites his cousin Daisy over to his home as per Gatsby's request.

• Gatsby and Daisy finally meet each other, and the intensity of Gatsby's love is evident to Nick.

CHAPTER 6

One day, a reporter lands in Gatsby's house enquiring if he has anything to say. Gatsby is confused, but it's apparent that the myths surrounding him have blown to huge proportions. Several rumors continue to float around, and some of them even suggest that he has a boat instead of a house and he secretly moves it up and down the island. James Gatz—Gatsby's original name—was born in North Dakota, and everything about him completely contrasts what he told Nick.

Nick recounts that James Gatz changed his fortune when he met a man named Dan Cody. Until then, James Gatz had been wandering around Minnesota trying to shape a persona he would later assume. Cody named him Jay Gatsby, but Nick feels that Gatsby had already decided his name before he even met Cody. Gatz was born in a very poor family and didn't think much of his parents' ability to succeed in their lives. He, however, had a vision of what he would become. But it was Cody who gave him the splendid opportunity to whet the fiction that would elucidate his life. Cody was about fifty years old, and as they traveled all over the continent, they became extremely close to each other. Their friendship would have progressed further had it not been for Cody's death.

Several days later, Nick goes to meet Gatsby in his house and is surprised to see Tom there. He has two other friends with him and, after conversing with a visibly unsettled Gatsby, he leaves with them. He mentions that he doesn't approve of Daisy's activities after Gatsby talks about Daisy. In fact, he becomes so curious about her that he lands at one of Gatsby's parties with her. Gatsby introduces them to all the celebrities present but subtly puts Tom in his place by referring to him as a polo player.

Daisy and Gatsby dance with each other and even spend some time alone on Nick's steps. Later, they return to the party and Daisy casually gives her husband a pen to ensure that he doesn't miss noting any woman's address. When the party's over and they all leave, Gatsby and Nick discuss the events of the evening. Nick cautions Gatsby that he shouldn't try to recreate the past. Gatsby insists that it's possible to do it, and Nick listens to him relating the events that occurred in the past between him and Daisy.

Key Takeaways

• Tom becomes suspicious of Daisy's activities and accompanies her to one of Gatsby's lavish parties.

• Gatsby dreams of recreating the past, and although Nick warns him against it, he doesn't pay any heed.

CHAPTER 7

Gatsby's parties suddenly stop out of the blue. He also replaces his servants to hide his secret with Daisy. Daisy invites Gatsby to lunch, and he turns up on an unbearably hot day. Tom, Daisy, Nick, Gatsby, and Jordan become increasingly uncomfortable as Daisy suggests that they all head out to town. Tom gets a phone call from his mistress, and this provokes Daisy to kiss Gatsby boldly. Tom is unaware of Daisy's love interests, but he witnesses Gatsby and Daisy exchanging glances with each other.

Tom's anger is palpable, but he decides to join them nonetheless. He grabs a whiskey bottle and they all leave their house. While Daisy and Gatsby travel in Tom's car, Jordan, Nick, and Tom drive in Tom's car. Tom notices that Gatsby's car is running low on gas, so he decides to stop by Wilson's garage. At that point, he's livid with anger because he has Gatsby investigated and learned that he's not what he claims to be.

Wilson appears to be extremely sick and declares that he's aware of Myrtle's love life. Of course, he doesn't know who she's having an affair with, but he tells Tom that he's leaving town with his wife. Within just an hour, Tom's forced to lose both his wife and mistress, and it upsets and angers him more than ever. As the group enters the Plaza Hotel, Tom seizes the opportunity to question Gatsby.

Gatsby stands his ground and reveals that Daisy only loves him and that she never loved Tom. Tom's furious and looks at Daisy for confirmation, but she's unable to honestly accept that she doesn't love Tom. Gatsby, panicking at the sudden development, tries a different tactic and announces that Daisy will leave Tom. Tom scoffs and responds by saying that she will never abandon him, especially for a bootlegger. Tom also orders Gatsby and Daisy to get back home in Gatsby's car, and they oblige.

At this point in time, Wilson, enraged by his wife's affairs, has her locked up in a room. Her neighbor frees her, but she blindly runs out on the road when she recognizes Tom's vehicle. Unfortunately, the car smashes her, and she dies instantly. Wilson is grief-stricken, and when Tom arrives on the scene, he's furious to learn that the car's description that killed Myrtle matches that of Gatsby's.

Later, Nick discerns that it was Daisy, not Gatsby who was driving the car. Gatsby is also ready to take all the blame for the unfortunate accident. In fact, his love for Daisy makes him stand guard in front of Daisy's house throughout the night. He's naturally worried that Tom might hurt Daisy, but Nick realizes that the reality is entirely different.

Key Takeaways

• Gatsby stops all his parties and reserves his time only for Daisy who boldly kisses him and claims that she loves him.

• Gatsby reveals Daisy's love in front of Tom, but she refuses to admit anything openly.

CHAPTER 8

Gatsby goes back home after spending the night in front of Daisy's house. Nick, feeling uneasy, tries to talk to him, but even he's unsure about how to communicate with Gatsby. It seems as if Gatsby has a hard time coming to terms with reality. Nick, on the other hand, is practical and tries to persuade Gatsby to leave the town. Gatsby assures him that there were no untoward incidents in Daisy's house, but Nick is persistent that he must protect himself. After all, the police could come searching for him any moment since his car was spotted at the location of the accident.

But, Gatsby is still stuck to his dream of leading a life with Daisy. Eager to share the details of his past, he reveals everything about his relationship with Daisy. This time, however, he's honest and tells Nick about how he and Daisy got intimate with each other. His intimacy made him feel like he was married to her. They were unequal when it came to their social status, yet they were deeply in love. Later, Gatsby left her to go to the war, but instead of returning home he went to Oxford, which made Daisy uncomfortable. She couldn't comprehend why Gatsby didn't return to her, and after waiting for a while, her interest began to fade, and she ultimately left him. She even wrote to Gatsby to inform him of her decision, but it was perhaps too late.

Gatsby returned to the United States and went in search of Daisy, but he learned that she was married and was on her honeymoon. The sudden turn of events left him shaken, and he began to chastise himself for not trying harder.

Gatsby continues to share intimate details, but the gardener suddenly appears and announces that he's going to drain away the pool. However, Gatsby tells him to wait since he wants to swim at least once before the summer is over.

Nick decides to leave and go back home, but he's uncomfortable about something. He isn't able to understand why he's feeling so, but a despondent feeling takes over him. Reluctantly, he leaves but not before telling Gatsby that he's worth more than all the other rotten people put together. On the other hand, Wilson, completely irrational after Myrtle's death, wants revenge and no amount of consoling helps. Tom tells him that Gatsby is responsible for his wife's demise and he heads towards Gatsby's house.

Nick feels restless at his office and decides to go home early since Gatsby fails to talk to him over the phone. Wilson finds Gatsby relaxing in his pool and shoots him without giving him a chance to react. Gatsby dies instantly, and Nick finds his lifeless body floating in his own swimming pool. At the same time, the gardener locates Wilson's body lying on the grass.

Key Takeaways

• Nick insists that Gatsby protects himself, but Gatsby is so hopeful of his future with Daisy that he refuses to budge.

• Tom tells Wilson that it was Gatsby who killed his wife and Wilson kills Gatsby in a fit of rage.

CHAPTER 9

After the paparazzi and police learn about Gatsby's death, they storm into his house. Nick grows increasingly uncomfortable with the knowledge that there's nobody to handle the funeral affairs. Convinced that Gatsby doesn't deserve to die alone, he calls Daisy, but he's told that Daisy and Tom are out on a trip. Nick grows more frustrated by the minute as he realizes that there's nobody to attend Gatsby's funeral.

Growing more restless, Nick phones Meyer Wolfshiem, but he also declines the invitation through a letter. At last, Nick calls Gatsby's father but doesn't unearth anything fruitful. Later, Klipspringer calls Nick, but Nick discerns that he's only calling to locate his tennis shoes. With no other option, Nick storms into Wolfshiem's office. However, Wolfshiem doesn't budge and declares that he only used Gatsby in numerous questionable activities. He states that Gatsby made his fortune only because of him, and Nick walks away, dejected yet furious at the turn of events.

Nick goes back to Gatsby's house and finds Gatsby's father—Mr. Gatz—strolling in the house. He takes in the surroundings and is proud of his son's achievements. Later, they head to the funeral, but there's nobody except the mail carrier and some servants. Nick is perturbed by the injustice meted out to such a fine man like Gatsby. In his heart, he believes that Gatsby was accused of things that weren't even faintly true. He begins to feel sick of all the rich people he has met and is struck by the horrific realization that not even a single person who used all of Gatsby's richness had bothered to come and attend his funeral.

Later, Jordan tries to talk to Nick, and although he's still fond of her, he simply dismisses her. He even notices Tom who comes to talk to him. Nick refuses even to shake his hand as he's disturbed by his behavior. It becomes clear that Tom is responsible for Gatsby's death, and Nick is so shattered and sorry that he sees no point in anything else. He realizes that careless people like Daisy and Tom simply break other people's lives and go back to their money as if nothing ever happened. Disgusted with everything, Nick goes to Gatsby's house and reminisces about the colorful parties that once took place in his home. He wonders about how Gatsby had given his everything to attain a distant dream—one that remained unfulfilled forever.

Key Takeaways

• Nick is struck by the fact that not even one person of all the people who enjoyed Gatsby's parties show up at his funeral.

• Nick is hurt and disgusted that Gatsby is accused of things that were absolutely untrue, and although he doesn't deserve it, he dies alone.

EDITORIAL REVIEW

The Great Gatsby is considered to be the best novel produced by Fitzgerald, and it's easy to understand why. What makes the book so spectacular is that it embodies the Jazz Age in all its glory. Set in the 1920s, the novel encapsulates the thoughts an entire generation during one of the most crucial periods witnessed in America. Jay Gatsby dreams to get his love back into his life and does everything he can to fulfill it.

Gatsby is so hopeful that he sees nothing else and weaves his entire life around Daisy. However, their social status doesn't match even when Gatsby is wealthy. While she comes from "old money" Gatsby is still considered worthless because of his "new money." Passionate about her, he calculates and plans everything, but fate has other plans for him. This story is about passion, money, lust, love, and relationships and it teaches how greed can destroy lives within a fraction of minutes.

ABOUT THE AUTHOR

F. Scott Fitzgerald, born on September 24, 1896, in Minnesota, had a troubled life even though he had a rare gift. At a very tender age, he began to write, but he took it seriously only after he joined the army since he was afraid that he would die before he could even publish his novel. He began working as a freelance writer and had some success; however, Fitzgerald gained more reputation as a playboy rather than a great writer when he was alive.

His works were successful, but he never tasted the success he deserved. He even tried to start a lucrative career in the field of advertising, but after his marriage, he quit his job and returned to writing. Once *The Great Gatsby* was published, Fitzgerald became famous, but the novel gained recognition as a classic piece of American fiction only after his death.

Unfortunately, Fitzgerald considered himself a failure even when he died. He suffered mental breakdowns and became a heavy drinker, but one can never deny the magic he wove in his books. He's remembered today even after a century because of his excellent choice of words and poetic style of writing.

LIST OF KEY CHARACTERS

Jay Gatsby – A self-made millionaire on a quest to live the American dream. His only dream is to reunite with the woman he lost long ago.

Nick Carraway – The narrator who has a house right next to Gatsby. He's also Daisy's cousin and plays a big role in reuniting Daisy and Gatsby.

Daisy Buchanan – Daisy is a rich, shallow young woman who suffers from an inability to understand others' emotions. Gatsby does everything for her, but she fails to return the favor.

Tom Buchanan – Tom is a pompous, muscular man who believes that he's superior to everybody else. Although he's Daisy's husband, he makes no efforts to change his brash, egoistic nature.

Jordan Baker – Jordan is a professional golfer who notoriously dishonest. She's also Daisy's friend, and she, just like Daisy, is very shallow and insensitive.

Myrtle Wilson – Myrtle is Tom's mistress who demands his attention. Tom treats her badly and also breaks her nose in a fit of anger, but that doesn't stop her from seeing him.

George Wilson – George is Myrtle's husband who is completely unaware of his wife's affair with Tom.

Catherine – Daisy's sister who doesn't have a say in anything. She's aware of Daisy's secrets and is happy to share the benefits.

Meyer Wolfshiem – Meyer is Gatsby's friend who claims to be Gatsby's benefactor, but he doesn't even turn up at his funeral.

Henry Gatz – Henry is Gatsby's father who comes to bury and pay his respects to his son.

SUBJECTIVE ANALYSIS

Nick Carraway, the narrator of the story, is Gatsby's neighbor and he witnesses everything that happens to Gatsby. Fitzgerald ensures that Nick's narrative is unbiased since he's able to analyze every situation with a balanced mind. He meets his cousin Daisy, but her luxurious life in East Egg is in complete contrast to his life in West Egg. While East Egg stands for old money that has been passed on from generations, West Egg houses people who have just scratched the surface of wealth and prosperity. Nick also has a wealthy background; however, it is nothing in comparison to Daisy's life filled with riches.

Nick meets Gatsby and finds that he's the most hopeful person he's ever met in his life. He observes Gatsby and is amused yet disconcerted by his behavior. He wants to trust Gatsby but is disappointed when he lies about his background. This gives the reader an inkling about Gatsby. Although he's amassed a lot of wealth, he's not really proud of what he's doing. His links with Meyer Wolfshiem makes his character even murkier, but once he confides everything in Nick, it becomes clear as to why he chose the path he did. Gatsby, desperate to gain Daisy's love does everything in his power to lure Daisy.

Nick finally realizes that Gatsby's every attempt to shape his life revolves around Daisy. Nick disapproves and tries to warn Gatsby. But Gatsby is so hopelessly in love that he fails to see the perils surrounding him. Perhaps, this is Fitzgerald's way of demonstrating that even extreme blind passion can trigger a chain of events that can unravel one's life. Love is an amazing feeling—a feeling to be cherished—but it's also imperative to be in touch with reality.

Gatsby could have accepted the truth about Daisy and moved on, but he was adamant about recreating the past. One thing led to another, and he couldn't get out of the web of destruction he had created around himself. He trusted Daisy that she wouldn't let him down, but ultimately his worst fears were confirmed. Gatsby held lavish parties that housed the entire town; however, not even a single stranger or friend turned up at his funeral. He died an untimely death he didn't deserve, but his obsessive love for Daisy had already stacked the cards of fate against him.

END

If you enjoyed this summary, please leave an honest review on Amazon.com!

If you haven't already, we encourage you to purchase a copy of the original book.

Made in the USA
San Bernardino, CA
22 August 2019